I0448542

One Team, One Mission, Securing Our Homeland

U.S. Department of Homeland Security Strategic Plan
Fiscal Years 2008–2013

 Homeland
Security

Letter from the Secretary

I am proud to present the *Department of Homeland Security (DHS) 2008 Strategic Plan*. This is the Department's second Strategic Plan, based on the overarching direction stated in the National Strategy for Homeland Security. With it, we will build on the progress we have made and define the successes we seek to achieve in the future. We have worked with determination to integrate the Department's varied elements; this new *Plan* charts a course to help further strengthen our efforts.

We are a unified Department with a shared focus: strengthening our Nation – through a partnership with individual citizens, the private sector, state, local, and tribal governments, and our global partners. We must also coordinate across Federal agencies, while shaping homeland security policy and coordinating incident management.

We seek continually to improve the operations of the Department, to discharge our duty of safeguarding the home front. This includes:

1. Clarifying, defining, and communicating leadership roles, responsibilities, and lines of authority at all government levels;

2. Strengthening accountability systems that balance the need for fast, flexible response with the need to prevent waste, fraud, and abuse;

3. Consolidating efforts to integrate the Department's critical mission of preparedness; and

4. Enhancing our capabilities to respond to major disasters and emergencies, including catastrophic events, particularly in terms of situational assessment and awareness, emergency communications, evacuations, search and rescue, logistics, and mass care and sheltering.

The *Second Stage Review (2SR)* process I ordered the Department to undertake in 2005 was designed to institutionalize the lessons learned since DHS was created in 2003. As a result of this review, we implemented a new management structure and philosophy. Because it is not feasible to secure our homeland against every conceivable threat, we have instituted risk management as the primary basis for policy and resource allocation decision making. Risk management assesses threats, vulnerabilities, and consequences, examines the best opportunities to mitigate risk, and provides a useful framework for obtaining and allocating the resources necessary to reduce risk to acceptable levels. We will anticipate emerging threats and take appropriate early action.

We must protect the homeland while also being prudent stewards of the resources provided by the American taxpayer. The Department must integrate sound practices from the private sector into the way we do business. My vision is to use those resources to recruit and retain a highly qualified professional workforce, and to deploy practical, cross functional strategies, policies, programs, resources, and technologies to fulfill our mission.

In these first years of the 21st century, America faces many challenges. But we have one particular competitive advantage: our resilience as a people. We have shown that when faced with adversity, we collectively possess both creativity and determination. I look forward to implementing this plan as a strong complement to our untiring American spirit.

One Team, One Mission, Securing Our Homeland

U.S. Department of Homeland Security Strategic Plan
Fiscal Years 2008–2013

Contents

I. Introduction

This Department of Homeland Security's overriding and urgent mission is to lead the unified national effort to secure the country and preserve our freedoms. While the Department was created to secure our country against those who seek to disrupt the American way of life, our charter also includes preparation for and response to all hazards and disasters. The citizens of the United States must have the utmost confidence that the Department can execute both of these missions.

The *2008 Strategic Plan* serves to focus the Department's mission and sharpen operational effectiveness, particularly in delivering services in support of Department-wide initiatives and the other mission goals. It identifies the goals and objectives by which we continually assess our performance. The Department uses performance measures at all levels to monitor our strategic progress and program success. This process also keeps the Department's priorities aligned, linking programs and operations to performance measures, mission goals, resource priorities, and strategic objectives.

Faced with the challenge of strengthening the components to function as a unified Department, DHS must coordinate centralized, integrated activities across components that are distinct in their missions and operations. Thus, sound and cohesive management is the key to Department-wide and component-level strategic goals. We seek to harmonize our efforts as we work diligently to accomplish our mission each and every day.

Americans are a resilient people. We have overcome great adversities in the past, and we will do so again. Regardless of what challenges may come, we will work tirelessly to protect our country. In the face of national challenges, we are one Nation. And here at DHS, we are one Department, unified to ensure the security of the American people – a Department that will continue striving to protect our homeland while ensuring the strength of our economy and pre-serving our cherished American freedoms and liberties.

In this spirit, it is important to acknowledge that this *Strategic Plan* is a living document and will be revised as needed to guide a dynamic Department and its ever-changing requirements.

II. Vision

A secure America, a confident public, and a strong and resilient society and economy.

III. Mission

We will lead the unified national effort to secure America. We will prevent and deter terrorist attacks and protect against and respond to threats and hazards to the Nation. We will secure our national borders while welcoming lawful immigrants, visitors, and trade.

IV. Core Values

Duty: Embodying Integrity, Responsibility, and Accountability.

We will faithfully execute the duties and responsibilities entrusted to us and maintain the highest ethical and professional standards. We will never forget that, for many, we are the face of America – the first Americans that many visitors will meet.

Respect: Honoring Our Partners and One Another.

We will highly value the relationships we build with our customers, partners, stakeholders, and each other. We will honor America's liberty, democracy, and diversity.

Innovation: Creating Opportunities.

We will identify and explore uncharted opportunities to enhance homeland security. We will encourage and recognize our employees' original thoughts and initiatives and will foster a creative environment in which they can grow, develop, and progress.

Vigilance: Safeguarding America.

We shall identify, defeat, and mitigate threats to the safety of the American people. We will constantly guard against threats, hazards, or other dangers that threaten our Nation and our way of life.

V. Guiding Principles

Protect Constitutional Rights and American Values.

We will always respect and preserve the individual rights enshrined in our Constitution and protect the privacy of our citizens and visitors.

Use an All-Hazards Approach.

Our Nation faces threats from both natural and man-made sources. We will take an all-hazards approach to emergency management that allows us to respond effectively to all emergencies, whether caused by acts of nature or by our enemies.

Build Trust through Collaboration and Partnerships.

We do not carry out the homeland security mission alone, and we can succeed only with the help of all levels of government, the private sector, academia, and the general public. We will be a trustworthy partner in building active layered defenses and national resilience. Through education and outreach, we will foster homeland security expertise across multiple disciplines to serve as an indispensable resource for the Nation. We will give Americans the tools they need to protect and help themselves and their neighbors in an emergency.

Apply Risk Management.

The homeland security mission is complex, and resources are constrained. The Department will use qualitative and quantitative risk assessments to inform resource decisions. These resources will be targeted at the most significant threats, vulnerabilities, and potential consequences.

Develop a Culture of Preparedness.

Disasters are a certainty, though when and where they will strike is unpredictable. This certainty should inform and motivate our preparedness. The Department will continue to foster a culture of preparedness throughout all levels of society and will emphasize the responsibility of the entire Nation to be flexible and capable of coping with a broad range of challenges.

Ensure Accountability.

Achieving our goals requires accountability through the human capital management system. This system will encourage innovation, recognition, mutual respect, and teamwork.

Capitalize on Emerging Technologies.

Innovations in science and technology will enable us to successfully execute the Department's missions. In addressing all our goals and objectives, we will use technology to enhance security and increase efficiency.

Work as an Integrated Response Team.

The Department was formed to unify the Federal Government's capacity to deal with terrorist attacks, major disasters, and other emergencies. By embracing a single set of guiding principles, from the Secretary to the frontline employee, we will forge a single entity working together to secure America.

The Department does not operate in a vacuum. Other Federal, State, local, and tribal institutions participate actively in the government's efforts to disrupt terrorist activities and in the preparation for and response to major disasters, as do our private and non-profit sectors and international partners. We will continue to work cooperatively to ensure that all of the instruments of national power – including leadership, specialized technical expertise, research, and development investments – are brought to bear on the challenges we face in a coordinated and unified manner.

Be Flexible.

Our security measures, preparedness, and response will always be capable of meeting diverse needs in a changing world. Our strategies will be flexible. We will be creative and nimble in defending the Nation against all threats. We will anticipate future threats and will not simply react to them once they have occurred. We will identify key factors external to the agency that could significantly affect the achievement of the general goals and objectives.

VI. Goals and Objectives

Protect Our Nation from Dangerous People

Strategic Goal 1

Objective 1.1

Achieve Effective Control of Our Borders.

We will reduce the likelihood that terrorists can enter the United States. We will strengthen our border security and gain effective control of our borders – at and between the ports, on land, at sea, and in the air. We will defend our homeland with layers of security. Whenever possible, we will expand our zone of security, managing risks and interdicting threats before they arrive on our shores. We will make our border security smarter, stronger, and more effective while facilitating legitimate travel, migration, and continued expansion of commerce.

Objective 1.2

Protect Our Interior and Enforce Immigration Laws.

We will increase the efficiency of our systems for processing arriving visitors and immigrants without sacrificing security or respect for human dignity. We will increase apprehensions of workers and employers violating immigration laws. We will administer immigration laws with integrity, efficiency, and respect.

Objective 1.3

Strengthen Screening of Travelers and Workers.

We will improve the security and mobility of travelers and increase focus on high-risk individuals through improved use of data, screening, fraud-resistant credentials, and biometric tools. This will reduce the risk of potential terrorism or other unlawful activities from threatening our Nation. We will streamline the screening of legitimate travelers and workers without sacrificing security. We will accomplish these protections while honoring the values that distinguish our country.

Objective 1.4

Improve Security through Enhanced Immigration Services.

We will increase our security by denying immigration benefits to persons wishing to do us harm and integrating our information with that of other Federal agencies with an aim of keeping out dangerous individuals. We will strengthen immigration fraud detection and other measures to protect the country while ensuring that we provide immigration benefits to eligible parties in a timely, efficient, and customer-centric manner.

Goal 1 Performance

Mission-oriented programs provide the means and strategies we use to achieve our goals and objectives. We quantitatively define outcomes and measure results using performance measures based on these programs. We continually strive to improve program alignment to our goals and objectives, and improve our performance measures.

DHS reports on program performance through a series of performance metrics. Below is a limited subset of our complete suite of measures, included here to provide a sense of how the Department tracks performance. The complete set of existing mission-oriented programs, performance measures, performance targets and results are reported in the *Annual Performance Report* (APR), available at *www.dhs.gov/xabout/budget/editorial_0430.shtm*.[1]

Select Reported Measures for Goal 1: Protect Our Nation from Dangerous People	
Measure	**FY 2013 Target**
Border miles under effective control (including certain coastal sectors).	*
Air Passenger Apprehension Rate for Major Violations. [Percent of the total number of individual passengers with major violations of customs and immigration laws and regulations that were apprehended based on statistical estimates of the total number of violations that came through our international airports.]	43.5%
Land Border Apprehension Rate for Major Violations. [Percent of the total number of vehicles travelers with major violations of customs and immigration laws and regulations that were apprehended based on statistical estimates of the total number of violations that came through the Points of Entry (POEs).]	37.5%
Percent of at-risk miles under strategic air surveillance.	95%
Percent of undocumented migrants who attempt to enter the U.S. via maritime routes that are interdicted. [As estimated, based upon data obtained from the U.S. Coast Guard and U.S. Customs and Border Protection.]	71.5%
Number of incursions into the U.S. exclusive economic zone (EEZ).	185
Percent of time that Coast Guard assets included in the Combatant Commander Operational Plans are ready at a Status of Resources and Training System (SORTS) rating of 2 or better.	100%
* The degree of effective control will be determined by the resources devoted to the task as developed in the Department's FY 2010-14 budget proposal and by funding provided by Congress.	

---

[1] The Fiscal Years 2007–2009 APR provides the mission oriented programs and performance measures according to the objective structure that was in place during FY 2007. The forthcoming FY 2008–10 APR will provide the programs and measures aligned to the goals and objectives reflected in this *Plan*.

Intentionally blank page. Please continue to the next page.

Protect Our Nation from Dangerous Goods

Strategic Goal 2

Objective 2.1

Prevent and Detect Radiological/Nuclear Attacks.

We will reduce the risk of, and guard against, nuclear and radiological attacks in the United States. We will develop and implement measures aimed at preventing successful introduction of nuclear and radiological weapons into the United States, whether by air, land, or sea. We will develop and deploy systems and intelligence capabilities – both domestically and overseas – to detect and prevent nuclear or radiological attacks at our borders or within our Nation.

Objective 2.2

Prevent, Detect, and Protect Against Biological Attacks.

We will lead efforts to establish an integrated National Bio-defense Architecture. We will systematically prioritize and focus efforts, including risk-based threat assessments, biological detectors, bio-surveillance, forensics, and emergency planning systems that can quickly detect, characterize, and respond to biological attack. We will prepare individuals, families, communities, and the Nation to respond effectively to biological attacks in the United States and minimize consequences.

Objective 2.3

Prevent and Detect Chemical and Explosive Attacks.

We will reduce the risk of and guard against chemical and explosive attacks in the United States. We will reduce the risks to our citizens and infrastructure from hazardous chemical and explosive attacks and incidents.

Objective 2.4

Prevent the Introduction of Illicit Contraband while Facilitating Trade.

We will guard against unlawful goods and activities entering the United States with minimal impact to legitimate trade. We will prohibit the introduction of illegal drugs and goods, and other harmful materials and organisms. We will partner with other agencies, foreign governments, and industry to share information and intelligence that will contribute to a safer America.

Goal 2 Performance

Mission-oriented programs provide the means and strategies we use to achieve our goals and objectives. We quantitatively define outcomes and measure results using performance measures based on these programs. We continually strive to improve program alignment to our goals and objectives, and improve our performance measures.

DHS reports on program performance through a series of performance metrics. Below is a limited subset of our complete suite of measures, included here to provide a sense of how the Department tracks performance. The complete set of existing mission-oriented programs, performance measures, performance targets and results are reported in the *Annual Performance Report* (APR), available at *www.dhs.gov/xabout/budget/editorial_0430.shtm*.[2]

<table>
<tr><td colspan="2">Select Reported Measures for Goal 2:
Protect our Nation from Dangerous Goods</td></tr>
<tr><td>Measure</td><td>FY 2013
Target</td></tr>
<tr><td>Percent of worldwide U.S. destined containers processed through Container Security Initiative (CSI) ports.</td><td>86%</td></tr>
<tr><td>Compliance rate of Customs-Trade Partnership Against Terrorism (C-TPAT) members with established C-TPAT security guidelines.</td><td>97%</td></tr>
<tr><td>Percent of border vehicle passengers in compliance with agricultural quarantine regulations.</td><td>95%</td></tr>
<tr><td>Removal rate for cocaine that is shipped via non-commercial maritime means. [Supply loss to smugglers relative to cocaine flow rate for the identified means.]</td><td>26.7%</td></tr>
<tr><td>Percent of the population in BioWatch jurisdictions covered by outdoor biological monitoring units.</td><td>SSI [3]</td></tr>
<tr><td>Percent of cargo, by volume, that passes through radiation portal monitors upon entering the Nation.</td><td>99%</td></tr>
</table>

---

[2] The Fiscal Years 2007–2009 APR provides the mission oriented programs and performance measures according to the objective structure that was in place during FY 2007. The forthcoming FY 2008–10 APR will provide the programs and measures aligned to the goals and objectives reflected in this Plan.

[3] SSI = Security Sensitive Information. The target is not made publicly available.

Intentionally blank page. Please continue to the next page.

Protect Critical Infrastructure

Strategic Goal 3

Objective 3.1

Protect and Strengthen the Resilience of the Nation's Critical Infrastructure and Key Resources.

We will lead the effort to mitigate potential vulnerabilities of our Nation's critical infrastructure and key resources to ensure its protection and resilience. We will foster mutually beneficial partnerships with public and private sector owners and operators to safeguard our critical infrastructure and key resources against the most dangerous threats and critical risks. We will strengthen resilience of critical infrastructure and key resources.

Objective 3.2

Ensure Continuity of Government Communications and Operations.

We will implement continuity of operations planning at key levels of government. We will improve our ability to continue performance of essential functions/business and government operations, including the protection of government personnel, facilities, national leaders, and the Nation's communications infrastructure across a wide range of potential emergencies.

Objective 3.3

Improve Cyber Security.

We will reduce our vulnerabilities to cyber system threats before they can be exploited to damage the Nation's critical infrastructures and ensure that such disruptions of cyberspace are infrequent, of minimal duration, manageable, and cause the least damage possible.

Objective 3.4

Protect Transportation Sectors.

We will improve the resilience and security of the domestic and intermodal transportation sectors including air cargo, passenger aviation, rail, transit, highways, maritime, and pipeline modes. We will strengthen the transportation network and effectively mitigate risk through an integrated systems approach that includes advancing foreign and domestic partnerships. We will continuously enhance marine safety and stewardship, including the safety of life at sea and protection of key resources.

Goal 3 Performance

Mission-oriented programs provide the means and strategies we use to achieve our goals and objectives. We quantitatively define outcomes and measure results using performance measures based on these programs. We continually strive to improve program alignment to our goals and objectives, and improve our performance measures.

DHS reports on program performance through a series of performance metrics. Below is a limited subset of our complete suite of measures, included here to provide a sense of how the Department tracks performance. The complete set of existing mission-oriented programs, performance measures, performance targets and results are reported in the *Annual Performance Report* (APR), available at *www.dhs.gov/xabout/budget/editorial_0430.shtm*.[4]

Select Reported Measures for Goal 3: Protect Critical Infrastructure	
Measure	**FY 2013 Target**
Percent of high priority Critical Infrastructure and Key Resources (CIKR) where a vulnerability assessment has been conducted and enhancement(s) have been implemented.	5%
Counterfeit passed as a percent of the amount of genuine currency in circulation.	< .0090%
Percentage of instances protectees arrive and depart safely.	100%
Percent of Federal Departments and Agencies with fully operational Continuity of Operations (COOP) capabilities.	100%
Percent reduction in the maritime terrorism risk over which the U.S. Coast Guard has influence.	25%
Critical infrastructure required visit rate.	100%
Priority Services call completion rate during emergency communications periods.	90%
Percent of airports in compliance with leading security indicators.	98%

---

[4] The Fiscal Years 2007–2009 APR provides the mission oriented programs and performance measures according to the objective structure that was in place during FY 2007. The forthcoming FY 2008–10 APR will provide the programs and measures aligned to the goals and objectives reflected in this *Plan*.

Intentionally blank page. Please continue to the next page.

Strengthen Our Nation's Preparedness and Emergency Response Capabilities

Strategic Goal 4

Objective 4.1

Ensure Preparedness.

We will empower Americans and governments at all levels to be prepared, capable, and ready to respond to adverse incidents. This national preparedness will help reduce the loss of life and property from adverse incidents, emergencies, and disasters, including catastrophic events by effectively preparing the Federal response and encouraging a national culture of preparedness and self-sufficiency. We will assist in providing for medical preparedness against public health threats – both naturally occurring and man-made. We will develop and employ joint planning and exercise capabilities to enhance governmental preparedness.

We will empower Americans to take individual and community actions before and after disaster strikes through effective mitigation and preparedness programs. We will ensure that Americans and their governments at all levels are ready for man-made events, natural disasters, and severe pandemics.

Objective 4.2

Strengthen Response and Recovery.

We will empower Americans and their governments at all levels to effectively respond to and recover from major disasters and emergencies, including catastrophic events. We will reduce the immediate loss of life and property from adverse incidents. We will work with our partners to help restore services and rebuild communities after incidents or emergencies.

We will strengthen nationwide response capabilities. We will act swiftly in response to a disaster, particularly when first responders are overwhelmed. We will deploy the necessary Departmental Components to assist those affected by a disaster. We will provide professional, trained, and certified leaders and staff to manage disaster relief and recovery operations, wherever they might occur.

We will build the foundation of an effective, coordinated response and define the doctrine to guide the national response. We will lead and sustain the Federal effort needed for disaster recovery while respecting and supporting the roles of individuals, State and local governments, faith-based and community organizations, and the private sector. We will increase our ability to deliver quick, compassionate, and easily accessed assistance to individuals and communities through the effective use of technology and streamlined, transparent processes while minimizing the occurrence of waste, fraud, and abuse.

Goal 4 Performance

Mission-oriented programs provide the means and strategies we use to achieve our goals and objectives. We quantitatively define outcomes and measure results using performance measures based on these programs. We continually strive to improve program alignment to our goals and objectives, and improve our performance measures.

DHS reports on program performance through a series of performance metrics. Below is a limited subset of our complete suite of measures, included here to provide a sense of how the Department tracks performance. The complete set of existing mission-oriented programs, performance measures, performance targets and results are reported in the *Annual Performance Report* (APR), available at *www.dhs.gov/xabout/budget/editorial_0430.shtm*.[5]

Select Reported Measures for Goal 4: Strengthen Our Nation's Preparedness and Emergency Response Capabilities	
Measure	**FY 2013 Target**
Percent of customers satisfied with Individual Recovery Assistance.	97%
Average time in hours to provide essential logistical services to an impacted community of 50,000 or fewer.	24 hours
Percent of response teams reported at operational status.	100%
Percent of Partner Organizations (POs) that respond "agree" or "strongly agree" that Federal Law Enforcement Training Center (FLETC) training programs address the right skills needed for their officers/agents to perform their law enforcement duties.	80%

---

[5] The Fiscal Years 2007–2009 APR provides the mission oriented programs and performance measures according to the objective structure that was in place during FY 2007. The forthcoming FY 2008–10 APR will provide the programs and measures aligned to the goals and objectives reflected in this Plan.

Intentionally blank page. Please continue to the next page.

Strengthen and Unify DHS Operations and Management

Strategic Goal 5

Objective 5.1

Improve Department Governance and Performance.

We will improve Department governance and performance in support of DHS Components delivering mission goals. We will lead efforts within the Department that provide structure to enhance Department-wide governance, decision making and oversight, including internal controls and performance management tracking. We will optimize processes and systems to facilitate integration and coordination. We will foster leadership to perform duties and effect progress while adhering to DHS core values and guiding principles. We will leverage culture to implement best practices that benefit from component commonalities and differences.

Objective 5.2

Advance Intelligence and Information Sharing.

We will ensure that timely, actionable, and complete intelligence and incident-related information reaches the right individuals at the right time to best mitigate threats and risk, while creating a culture of awareness for privacy, civil liberties, and civil rights. We will work to maximize the value of this information to those who receive it.

We will ensure that the DHS culture, business processes, and governance employ the broadest possible structure to collect, communicate, analyze, disseminate, and integrate homeland security and law enforcement intelligence and information. We will improve interaction between disparate systems, align shared services, and build sustainable information sharing infrastructures. We will enhance integration among the intelligence components of the Department, using standardized processes that support a unified DHS intelligence mission that epitomizes a streamlined model of efficiency.

As we advance information sharing partnerships, we will collaborate closely and work to identify and minimize barriers to sharing information among Federal, State, local, tribal, international, and private and non-profit sector security partners. We will ensure that our domestic and international partners receive needed risk information and share their information with the Federal Government. We will continuously assess our work to enhance our performance in sharing and analyzing intelligence and information.

Objective 5.3

Integrate DHS Policy, Planning, and Operations Coordination.

We will strengthen and unify strategic and policy direction through improved strategic planning and assessment. We will ensure that these efforts are integrated with and informed by the Department's operations coordination and planning efforts. We will create and enhance a DHS operations coordination capability to plan for and coordinate non-routine, cross-cutting operations that require multi-Component activities.

Goal 5 Performance

Mission-oriented programs provide the means and strategies we use to achieve our goals and objectives. We quantitatively define outcomes and measure results using performance measures based on these programs. We continually strive to improve program alignment to our goals and objectives, and improve our performance measures.

DHS reports on program performance through a series of performance metrics. Below is a limited subset of our complete suite of measures, included here to provide a sense of how the Department tracks performance. The complete set of existing mission-oriented programs, performance measures, performance targets and results are reported in the *Annual Performance Report* (APR), available at *www.dhs.gov/xabout/budget/editorial_0430.shtm*.[6]

Select Reported Measures for Goal 5: Strengthen and Unify DHS Operations and Management	
Measure	**FY 2013 Target**
Percent of the President's Management Agenda Initiatives that receive a green progress score from the Office of Management and Budget.	87%
Total instances of material weakness conditions identified by the independent auditor in their report on the DHS financial statements.	<8
Percent of favorable responses by DHS employees on the Federal Human Capital Survey.	58% [7]
Number of Homeland Intelligence Reports (HIRs) disseminated.	3,065
Percent of active Homeland Security Information Network (HSIN) users.	95%
Percent of component-to-component information sharing relationships documented through information sharing and access agreements (ISAAs).	95%

---

[6] The Fiscal Years 2007–2009 APR provides the mission oriented programs and performance measures according to the objective structure that was in place during FY 2007. The forthcoming FY 2008–10 APR will provide the programs and measures aligned to the goals and objectives reflected in this *Plan*.

[7] 58% is the stated target for FY 2012. The Federal Human Capital Survey is a biennial survey conducted in even numbered years. There is no FY 2013 target.

Appendix A: Linking Strategy and Performance

DHS is committed to strengthening our ability to report on performance results in achieving our goals and delivering value to the American public. The Department's efforts are guided by the *Government Performance and Results Act of 1993* (GPRA), which focuses on Federal management and accountability with an emphasis on outcomes and reporting on the degree to which goals are met.

DHS Performance Management Framework

Figure 1 presents the DHS performance management framework used to tie Department-wide goals and objectives to mission-oriented programs, and their associated program performance goals and performance measures. Below is the index of terms used in the DHS Performance Management Framework.

Figure 1

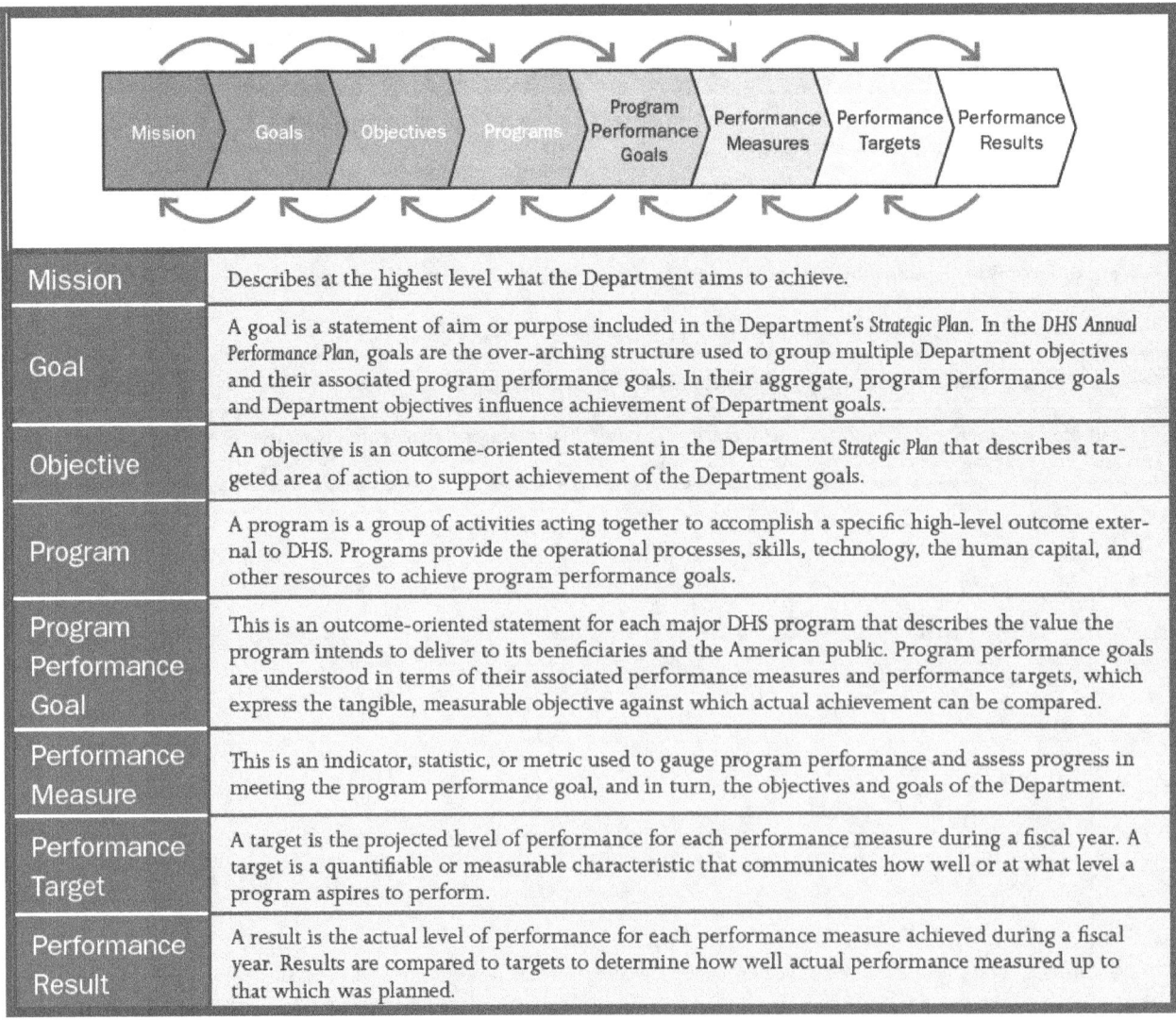

Mission	Describes at the highest level what the Department aims to achieve.
Goal	A goal is a statement of aim or purpose included in the Department's *Strategic Plan*. In the DHS *Annual Performance Plan*, goals are the over-arching structure used to group multiple Department objectives and their associated program performance goals. In their aggregate, program performance goals and Department objectives influence achievement of Department goals.
Objective	An objective is an outcome-oriented statement in the Department *Strategic Plan* that describes a targeted area of action to support achievement of the Department goals.
Program	A program is a group of activities acting together to accomplish a specific high-level outcome external to DHS. Programs provide the operational processes, skills, technology, the human capital, and other resources to achieve program performance goals.
Program Performance Goal	This is an outcome-oriented statement for each major DHS program that describes the value the program intends to deliver to its beneficiaries and the American public. Program performance goals are understood in terms of their associated performance measures and performance targets, which express the tangible, measurable objective against which actual achievement can be compared.
Performance Measure	This is an indicator, statistic, or metric used to gauge program performance and assess progress in meeting the program performance goal, and in turn, the objectives and goals of the Department.
Performance Target	A target is the projected level of performance for each performance measure during a fiscal year. A target is a quantifiable or measurable characteristic that communicates how well or at what level a program aspires to perform.
Performance Result	A result is the actual level of performance for each performance measure achieved during a fiscal year. Results are compared to targets to determine how well actual performance measured up to that which was planned.

The Department uses performance measures at all levels to monitor progress in achieving its *Strategic Plan* and attaining program success. The long-term program performance goal established for each DHS program provides the basis for assessing contributions to achievement of Department strategic goals and objectives. Thus, individual program performance results are tied to strategic level goals and objectives which are aligned with the Department's mission.

A variety of measures are reported publicly to the President, Congress, and the American people to indicate DHS achievements, while other measures are used internally to manage the activities of DHS programs. The *Future Years' Homeland Security Program* (FYHSP), the DHS *2008 Strategic Plan*, and *DHS Annual Performance Report* provide key management and reporting mechanisms by which the Department implements its performance management framework to assess accomplishments of Department strategic objectives and goals.

The *Homeland Security Act of 2002* requires DHS to annually update and maintain a current FYHSP. The FYHSP details our five-year program resource and performance plans to meet DHS strategic goals and objectives – the FYHSP is the embodiment of the *DHS Strategic Plan*. In conjunction with developing the FYHSP, DHS compiles its *Annual Performance Report* so as to comply with the GPRA and *Office of Management and Budget (OMB) Circular A-11*. Annual reports linking DHS actual and planned performance levels and metrics, the *Strategic Plan* and long-term goals can be found at *www.dhs.gov/xabout/*.

Performance measures included in the performance plan are tracked on a quarterly basis to provide a trend toward meeting annual targets. Program managers provide data that is summarized in the *DHS Quarterly Performance Report*. This quarterly assessment not only provides actual performance data to date, but it also provides an assessment by program managers of whether they believe they are going to achieve their targets by the end of the fiscal year. If it appears that target may not be met, program managers are encouraged to initiate corrective actions to address program performance. The *DHS Quarterly Performance Report* also summarizes performance related information associated with *OMB's Program Assessment Rating Tool* (PART) and the *President's Management Agenda* (PMA).

In addition to this framework, which is currently focused largely on the individual program level, DHS is developing strategic outcome measures to measure Departmental progress in achieving its strategic objectives. These strategic outcome measures are derived by aggregating current GPRA performance measures and proposed future measures. Examples are provided in the "Goals and Objectives" section of this *Strategic Plan*.

External Challenges

The Department of Homeland Security has a critical role in securing our Homeland, yet the nature of American society and the structure of American governance make it difficult to achieve the goals of a secure homeland through the Department of Homeland Security alone.

Trying to protect every person from every threat at every moment would be at a tremendous cost to our freedoms, our economy, and our way of life. Our challenge is to manage risk, consistent with an understanding of threats, vulnerabilities, and consequences by prioritizing our resources to prepare for high-risk scenarios. The Department's approach to homeland security requires shared responsibility and partnership with Congress; other Federal agencies, State, local, and tribal governments; the private sector; the American people; and our international partners. We need others to assist us to meet our goals in securing the Nation.

Our effort to protect our Nation from dangerous people and goods depends in part upon assistance from our international partners, particularly in the areas of achieving effective control of our borders and the screening of international travelers and goods. Negative impacts on continued international cooperation could seriously challenge our ability to meet these goals.

Similarly, a worsening in global economic conditions, particularly in the Western Hemisphere, could provide additional impetus to illegal immigration, making our effort to protect our interior and enforce immigration laws more difficult. These same possible economic conditions could also impact the Federal budget: the Department's secure border programs, for example, depend significantly upon the continuance of full resource support to achieve results by adding new Border Patrol Agents, enhancing interior enforcement efforts, providing for specific Secure Border Initiative elements such as fencing and other infrastructure improvements, adding new U.S. Customs and Border Protection Officers for the many ports of entry, and modernizing the ports of entry.

Technological and social changes present a special challenge. An unfortunate consequence of living in a networked, technologically dependent world is that terrorists seek to use our own technology against us. There is the possibility that our adversaries will be able to surprise us particularly with rapid advances in biotechnology and threats to cyberspace that would inhibit our ability to protect the Nation. On the social front, groups of American-born citizens that now may hold radical beliefs, but appear to be non-violent, could change their strategy and adopt violence to achieve political ends, requiring a greater focus of efforts broader than to secure the border, screen travelers and improve security through enhanced immigration services.

Some external threats we can prevent from coming to fruition, but some we cannot. However, those threats unleashed by nature are the hardest to prevent. Significant challenges remain in building a national "culture of preparedness" that is founded on individual and community preparedness and responsibility. The American public has an increasing expectation of the Federal Government's role in disaster response and recovery that is not always balanced with the need for personal and community responsibility, and that can eclipse the primary role of the State and local governments in preparedness and response. Building an effective national emergency response system will entail continuing efforts to develop and sustain national partnerships across all levels of government, voluntary organizations, and the private sector, which ensure active and trusted working relationships during periods of high-stress disaster activity.

Finally, as an "enabling" goal, we seek to unify our Department's operations and management. We continue to plan for the move of our Component offices to the St. Elizabeth's Campus in Washington, D.C., which is the first critical step toward a consolidated DHS Headquarters. We will face budgetary, environmental, and historical preservation challenges. External support from the local community and other Federal agencies will be needed to fulfill this critical element of our effort to strengthen and unify the Department of Homeland Security.

Intentionally blank page. Please continue to the next page.

Appendix B: Strategic Context and Stakeholder Outreach

Strategic Context

The DHS *2008 Strategic Plan* considers a multitude of internal and external forces likely to shape current and future challenges to our Nation's people, society, and economy. The *Plan* also considers how these forces may affect the United States' role in the world, as well as the roles that Federal, State, local, and tribal governments, and the private sector play in securing the homeland. For an independent assessment of how DHS might operate in the coming years, the Office of Strategic Plans commissioned a detailed report by the Homeland Security Institute (HSI), the Department's federally-funded research and development center. The HSI report's findings highlight a number of themes that will affect the Department – themes that complement many existing Presidential Directives and national strategies.

The assessment identifies the two principal sources of risk our Nation faces – dangers posed by human architects or by nature. It also identifies a number of factors that could influence the environment in which the Department operates. First, the report considers it likely that nation-states will continue as the dominant players on the world stage. It also envisages, however, that governments will have less control over information, technology, disease, and migrants, and that the global community will continue to exist in a profound sense of uncertainty. The report indicates that non-state actors will likely play a larger role, to both positive and negative ends, in influencing the global framework. The report also concludes that greater inter-connectivity and networks will provide opportunities for transnational criminals.

The HSI assessment develops nine themes that will affect future homeland security decision-making. The themes are consistent with contemporary thinking on issues of national significance and do not recommend drastic departures from current homeland security planning; they do confirm the importance of the priorities the Secretary and senior leadership identified in addressing the challenges of the coming years. These themes are:

- Increasing global interdependence of economies, enterprises, and governments;
- Threats from domestic and transnational terrorists;
- Challenges to U.S. homeland security emanating from nation-states;
- Impact of transnational criminal networks;
- Outbreak and rapid spread of virulent diseases;
- Effect of large-scale natural disasters;
- Proliferation and acquisition of weapons of mass destruction;
- Advances in scientific knowledge and applications and resultant challenges and opportunities; and
- Physical and cyber critical infrastructure in the United States.

A second analytical effort also helped develop the strategic context in which future homeland security decisions will be made. "Project Horizon" was a strategic process used by Federal

Government agencies in the spring of 2006. It identified a set of complex global conditions that could emerge by 2025. Recommendations from HSI and the "Project Horizon" core team reinforce the need for homeland security plans to be flexible and for homeland security organizations to be agile in their thinking.

Stakeholder Outreach

The Department of Homeland Security cannot consider its long-term homeland security strategy in a vacuum. With so many critical stakeholders in Federal, State, local, tribal governments, the private sector, and within academia, it was essential for the Department to solicit external input for the development of this *Plan*.

To gain the broadest possible feedback, the Department mounted an expansive outreach effort to better understand the strengths and weaknesses of the *2004 Strategic Plan*, as well as potential areas of improvement. Working with the Private Sector Office, the Homeland Security Advisory Council, and the Office of Intergovernmental Programs, the Department's Office of Strategic Plans solicited the input from a wide variety of governmental, non-profit, and private sector organizations.

Given the range of perspectives and expertise among Department headquarters and agencies, the Office of Strategic Plans additionally conducted a series of workshops as part of its strategic planning process. Subject matter experts from all the Department's Component agencies participated actively in a truly collaborative process; as a result, we were able to integrate key elements from the input into this new version.

The Department also acknowledged the importance of its sister agencies in achieving its strategic goals by soliciting comments from key partners regarding the *Strategic Plan*, including the U.S. Department of Defense, the U.S. Department of State, the Office of Management and Budget, the Government Accountability Office, and HSI. These organizations provided a wide range of valuable insights and suggestions for inclusion in the *Plan*.

Appendix C: Planning Process

DHS Strategic Plan Development

The DHS Office of Strategic Plans provides a central focus for the formulation of Department-wide, long-range planning and strategic goals to safeguard the homeland. The Office of Strategic Plans uses a strategic planning process that considers the homeland security environment details, plans, authorities, reports, studies, and analysis of the current and future challenges facing DHS and the strategic vision for its future. The *Strategic Plan* addresses the present needs of DHS, as well as those that may arise in the complex homeland security arena over the next 5 years. Figure 2 illustrates the process flow for strategic plan development that is discussed below.

Figure 2

DHS Strategic Plan Structure

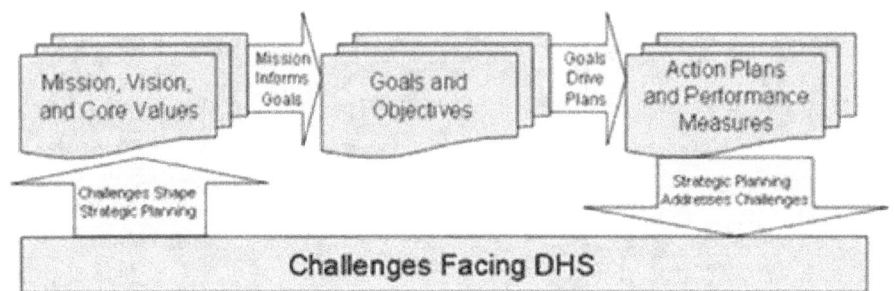

In support of the development of the *DHS Strategic Plan*, the Office of Strategic Plans conducted an assessment of the challenges and strategic issues facing DHS during the next 10 years. Through analysis of the challenges, DHS plans, DHS policies, governmental guidance, and executive level priorities, Office of Strategic Plans developed an initial mission statement, vision, and core values. Working groups, consisting of representatives from across DHS, validated this comprehensive statement of DHS's purpose, image of its future, and characteristics. The DHS participants reviewed goals and objectives that reflect the desired state of DHS in the next 10 years. They endorsed five core goals and multiple objectives that the Department aims to accomplish.

Strategic goals and objectives provide overarching guidance for executing the Department's mission. Well-defined desired strategic outcomes provide the means to assess whether the strategic goals and objectives are being met. Coordinated strategic and program performance measures enable overall organizational assessment of the Department's efforts towards its desired mission accomplishments.

Figure 3 shows an overview of the DHS strategic planning landscape integrated with the DHS Planning, Programming, Budgeting, and Execution Cycle.

Figure 3

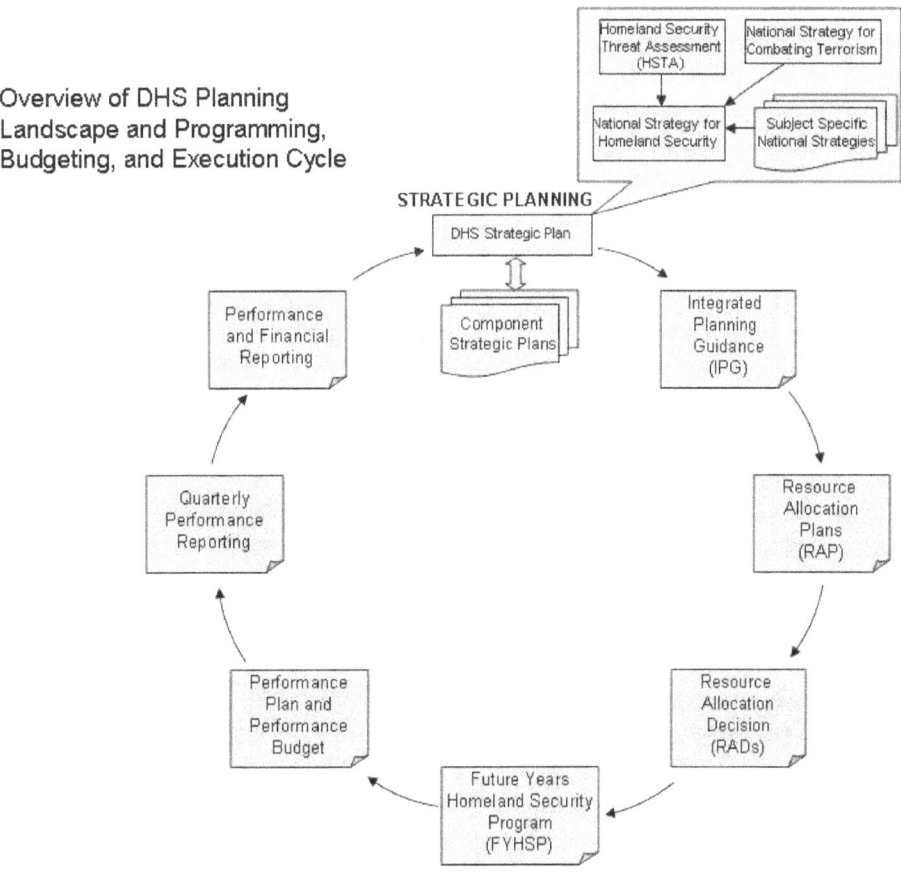

Overview of DHS Planning
Landscape and Programming,
Budgeting, and Execution Cycle

DHS Planning, Programming, Budgeting, and Execution Process

DHS uses the *Planning, Programming, Budgeting, and Execution* (PPBE) process to determine priorities and allocate resources. In *Planning*, risk assessment and mission scoping are conducted to determine and prioritize the capabilities necessary to meet the needs of the Department that are presented in the *DHS Strategic Plan*. In *Programming*, resources are allocated to best meet the prioritized needs within projected resource constraints. In *Budgeting*, detailed budget estimates are developed ensuring that the most efficient use of limited funding and that priorities are being met as effectively as possible. Finally, in *Execution*, program execution and output are assessed against planned performance and strategic progression to determine the best return on investment.

The Office of Strategic Plans is responsible for the development and alignment of the Department's long-term goals and objectives. Overarching guidance is provided by the National Strategy for Homeland Security, which is the foundation for the *DHS Strategic Plan*. Office of Strategic Plans assists DHS areas in developing, aligning, and assessing their mid- to long-range planning initiatives with the *DHS Strategic Plan* and other high-level policy documents.

The Integrated Planning Guidance (IPG) is an internal planning document developed each year to articulate the Secretary's investment priorities, which are developed through a combination of congressional and executive mandates and risk assessments. These priorities inform the preparation of annual and five-year budget plans. *The Resource Allocation Plan* (RAP) assists the Secretary of Homeland Security with investment and divestment decisions. This process represents the first step of a continuous cycle of mission execution and evaluation, and clearly links the broader framework of Department goals and objectives to specific investments and allocations. Figures 4 and 5 below provide an overview of the phases of the DHS PPBE process.

Figure 4

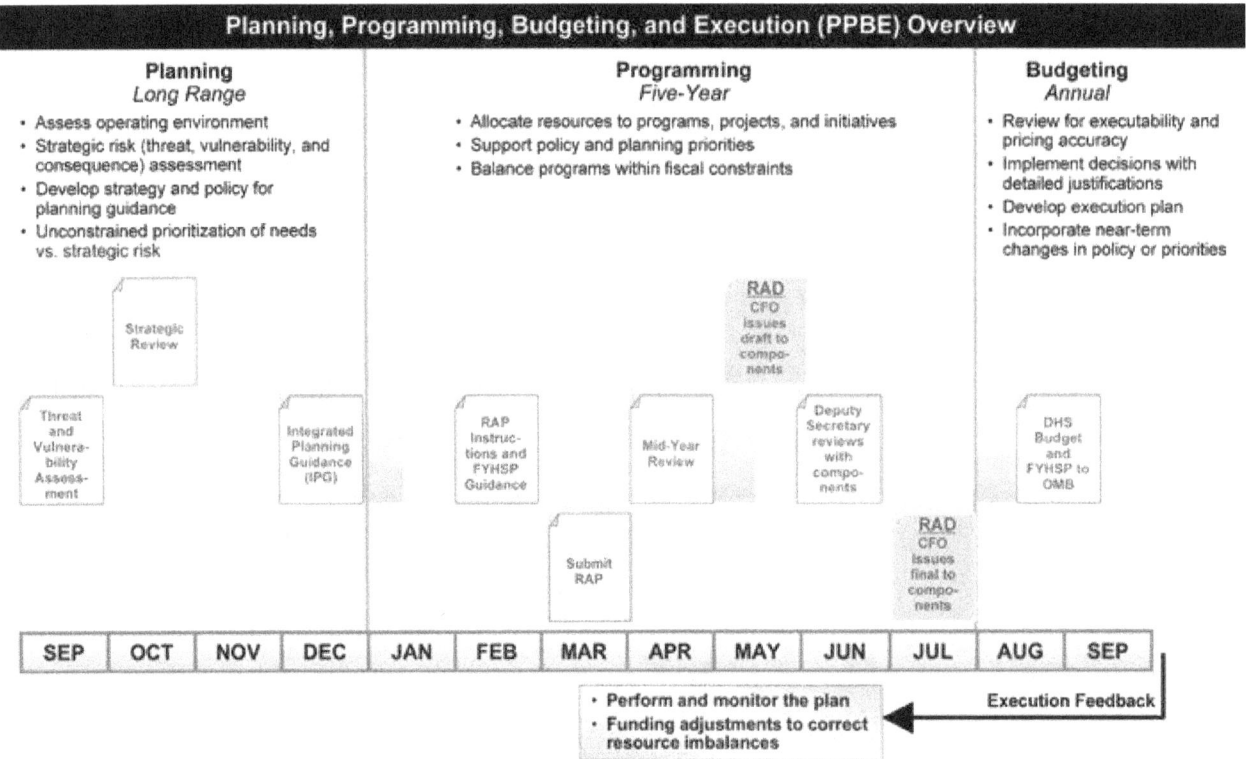

The Office of Program Analysis & Evaluation oversees the integration of the PPBE process and serves as the Department's primary source of program analysis and evaluation. During the programming phase, they help ensure DHS resource plans are meeting goals and objectives, simultaneously considering alternative methods of accomplishing them based upon fiscal management, and monitoring each program's success at achieving these priorities. Figure 5 below depicts the overlapping cycles of the PPBE process over a given fiscal year.

The process culminates in the annual development of the Department's FYHSP. The FYHSP, mandated by Congress, expresses the Secretary's five-year strategic resource allocation intentions, and connects the multi-year spending priorities of each program in the Department with the achievement of the goals and objectives of the *DHS Strategic Plan*.

Figure 5

Planning, Programming, Budgeting and Execution
Overlapping Cycles

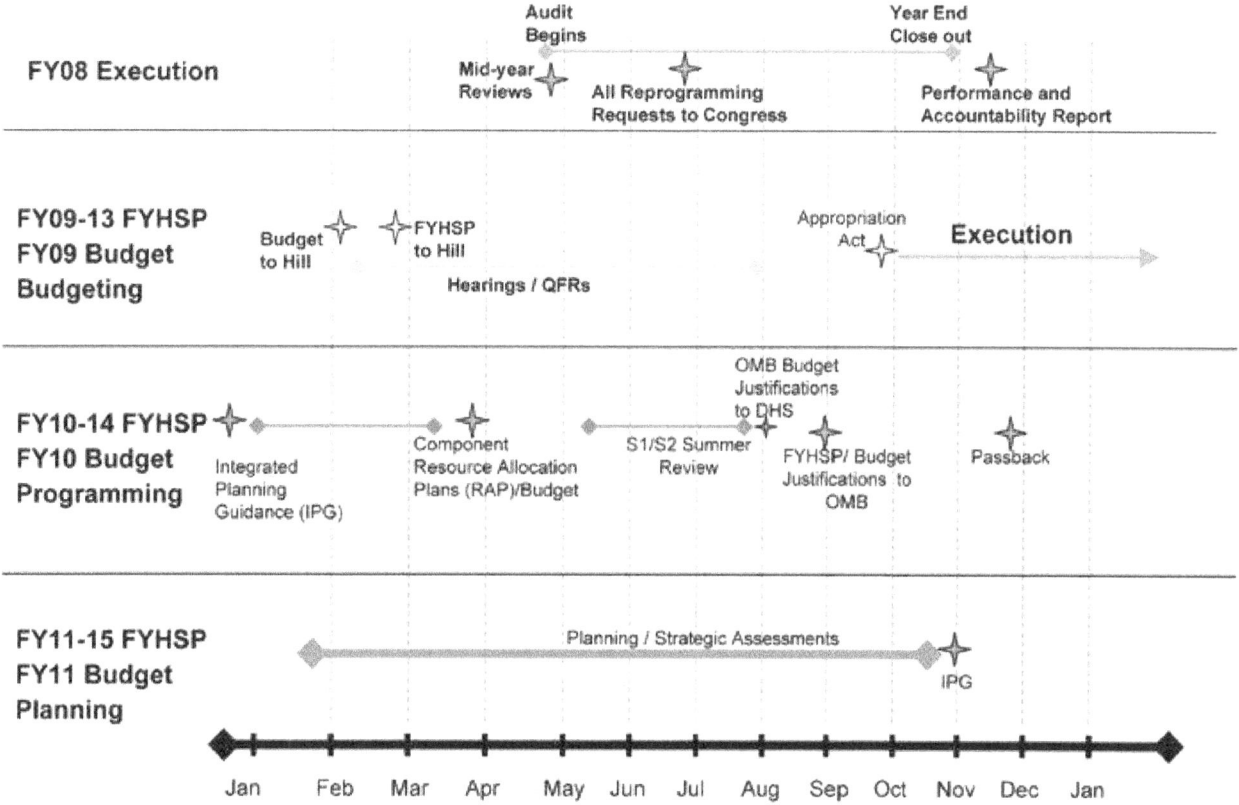

Evaluations Considered in Establishing Goals and Objectives

FYHSP performance information played an integral part in the development of the *Strategic Plan*. The Department uses a variety of program evaluation tools to assess program effectiveness and efficiency, including the OMB PART and the *President's Management Agenda* (PMA). PART is used to assess the strengths and weaknesses of DHS's FYHSP programs, and evaluates each program's purpose and performance results. PART evaluations are conducted in accordance with a schedule coordinated with OMB.

Most notably, a total of 65 OMB PART program evaluations have been conducted, highlighting for each DHS program its purpose, design, and long-term annual measures and targets. Strategic planning efforts to develop valid long-term and annual measures and targets, including financial oversight and program improvement effort are also rated. Having this level of program detail was instrumental in clarifying key homeland security programs, resources, and tools designed to implement our mission and goals.

While some DHS programs are new and working to establish sound performance measures with multi-year data, the majority of the programs have scored well in terms of program purpose, design, and strategic planning. This insight is also considered when developing the Department's *Strategic Plan*.

Similarly, the PMA is used to assess progress being made in achieving standards the President has specified in a number of management initiative areas, including: strategic management of human capital, competitive sourcing, improved financial performance, expanded electronic government, and budget and performance integration. Each management initiative area is scored quarterly, for DHS as a whole by OMB, and for DHS agencies by headquarters.

Schedule for Future Program Evaluations

The Department continuously reports, at the program level, the results of program and management assessments to OMB, Congress, and taxpayers, who expect us to achieve our mission. The *Performance Budget*, submitted annually to justify budget requests, includes program performance metrics that link program resource allocations with strategic results. *The Quarterly Performance Report* provides DHS leadership a quarterly summary of the achievement of these results, with performance measures, PART results, PMA scores, and progress made on each of the Secretary's priorities. Finally, the PAR, submitted annually to Congress, reports annual results.

While each DHS agency works to implement specific plans for future program evaluations, DHS will continue to participate in the PART process as the government-wide means of conducting thorough program evaluations. Future PART program evaluation schedules are developed in concert with OMB and will focus on those programs that in the past have been unable to demonstrate results due to the lack of performance measures and multi-year actual data. In addition, new programs that emerge to address mission-oriented needs will be evaluated through the PART process.

Intentionally blank page. Please continue to the next page.

Appendix D: DHS Organizational Chart

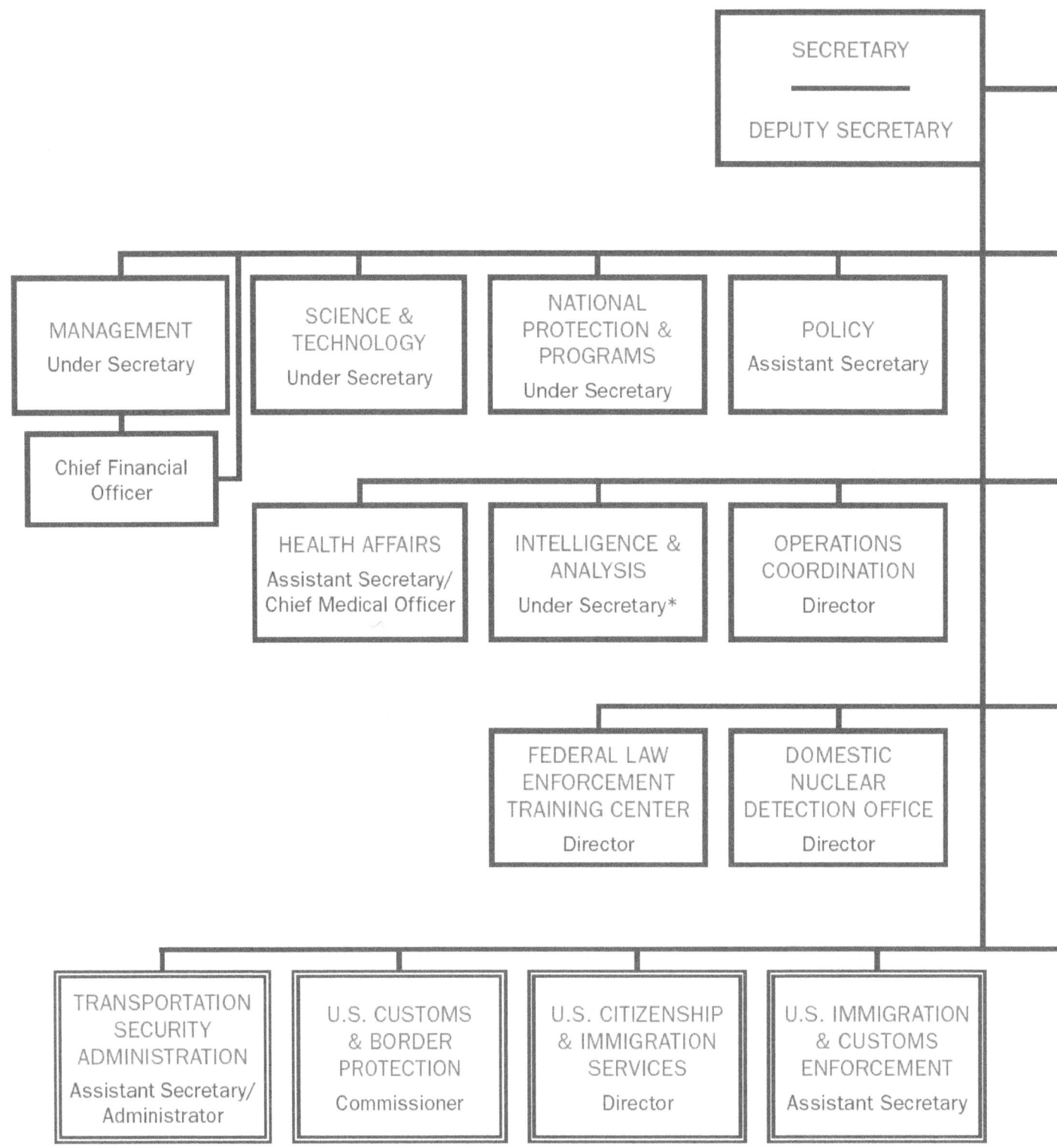

* Under Secretary for Intelligence & Analysis title created by Public Law 110–53, August 3, 2007.

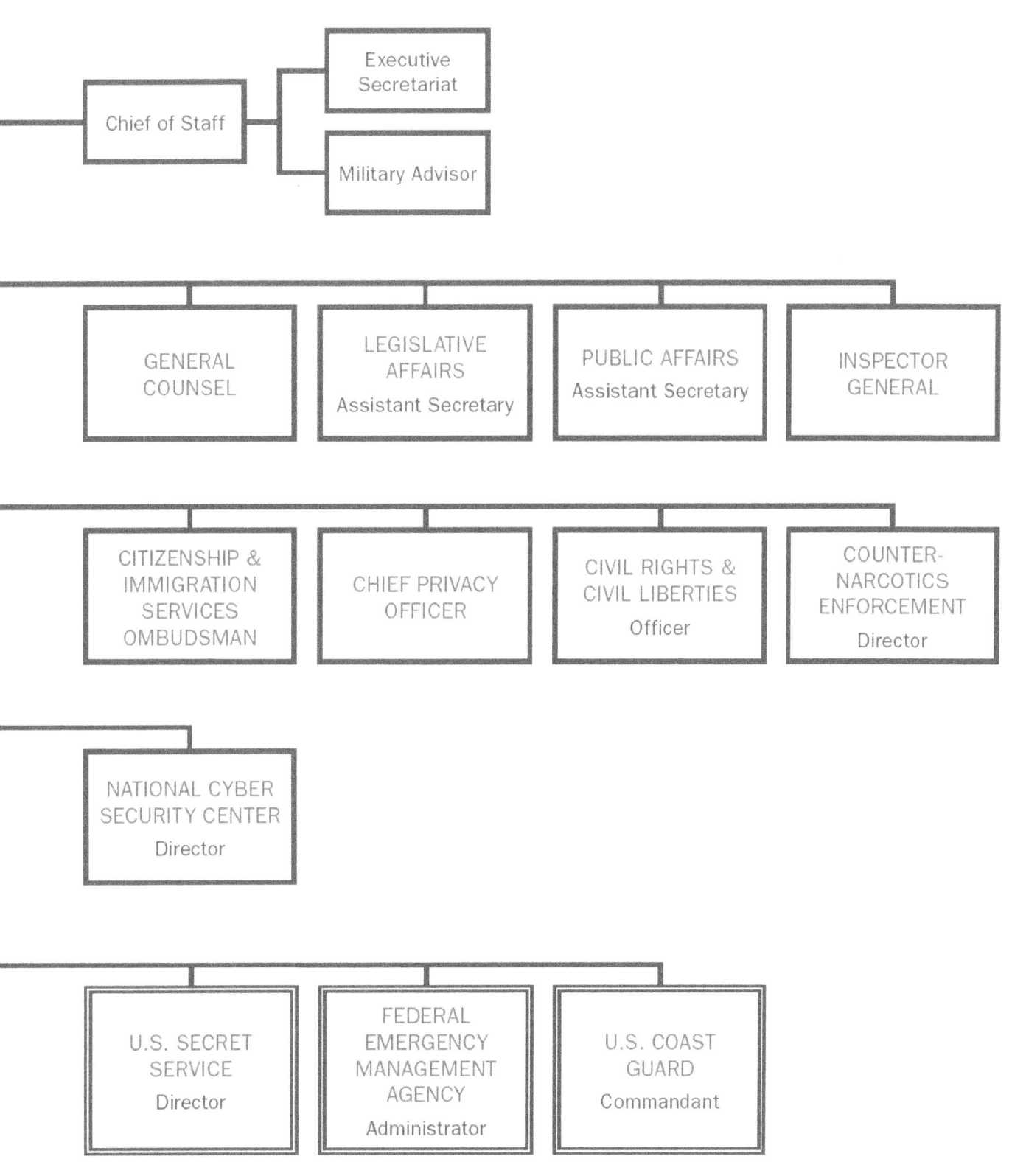

Chief of Staff

Executive Secretariat

Military Advisor

GENERAL COUNSEL

LEGISLATIVE AFFAIRS
Assistant Secretary

PUBLIC AFFAIRS
Assistant Secretary

INSPECTOR GENERAL

CITIZENSHIP & IMMIGRATION SERVICES OMBUDSMAN

CHIEF PRIVACY OFFICER

CIVIL RIGHTS & CIVIL LIBERTIES
Officer

COUNTER-NARCOTICS ENFORCEMENT
Director

NATIONAL CYBER SECURITY CENTER
Director

U.S. SECRET SERVICE
Director

FEDERAL EMERGENCY MANAGEMENT AGENCY
Administrator

U.S. COAST GUARD
Commandant

Approved 3/20/2008

www.ingramcontent.com/pod-product-compliance
Lightning Source LLC
Chambersburg PA
CBHW080634290526
45790CB00007B/3055